From The Ashes

My Journey From Extreme Sexual Abuse To Wholeness

Stephanie L. Giaquinto

Copyright © 2014 Stephanie L. Giaquinto
All rights reserved

ISBN: 1495908860
ISBN 13: 9781495908866
Library of Congress Control Number: 2014902891
CreateSpace Independent Publishing Platform
North Charleston, South Carolina

This book is dedicated to Karl, who showed me the way,
And to John, who loves me without reservation.

THIS MAY BE TRIGGERING FOR ABUSE SURVIVORS.
Please take good care of yourself while reading and reach out
for support if needed.

Introduction

Most people don't know this about me. For the first six years of my life, I lived in routine horror. My father and some paternal relatives were members of a local crime ring affiliated with larger ones in nearby cities. My father kept my mother under his thumb. I suffered sadistic abuse as "training" for membership. One job for which I was groomed was prostitute. My perpetrators needed to break my fragile self in order to mold me into a willing slave. Often I sat alone, naked, in a basement room. It was a concrete prison with one small window. I was deprived of my needs. I had comforting fantasies of my father rescuing me from my emptiness and shame. Inevitably, he would return, my savior and my worst nightmare. I both worshipped and despised him.

I was repeatedly raped. I would scream, and the men would laugh. When I'd cry, they'd increase the torture. In every way, and through every means, they broke me. They taught me to seduce men. The sense of power was heady. I was officially "turned out" at the age of four. I disowned the broken, disparate parts of me, and I mistook the abuse for love.

For years, after my mother and I escaped my father, I suffered with aftereffects, including a powerful addiction to sex (both fantasy and action) and "love", or emotional dependency.

In 1996, I began receiving good therapy. I spent years arduously putting Humpty together again. Eventually, I became a member of SLAA, Sex and Love Addicts Anonymous. I came to experience the love of a good man. And I found faith in a God of my understanding.

I still bear some scars. But every time I choose to act from a place of love and kindness, I win.

This is my story. I hope it speaks to you. I've included some helpful links in the back of the book for those still suffering.

It gets better. I promise.

I Was Raped

I was raped last night
And now the sky is green, and the grass is blue.
My heart is broken, and my inside is gone.
What do I do without an inside?
I was raped last night
And I hurt.
I should smile.
I don't want to smile.
I have an eternity's worth of tears hidden behind my eyes.
I am seeing blood.
I don't want you to look at me.
Go away, and leave me alone.
I am alone in a room full of people.
I want to moan.
I must be quiet.
I was raped last night
And life goes on.
Why don't people notice that the world is upside down?
My body aches.
My life is altered.
I see you laughing.
You look so happy.
But I'm laughing, too
So were you raped last night?
I was raped last night
And I don't need anyone
And I need everyone.
Men become monsters
And men become mirrors
And I try to enslave men with my sexuality.

I cannot make love, only sex.
I lost my body
And the very thing that hurt is what I seek.
I was raped last night
And the dark closes in and chokes me
And I have no feelings
And I am nothing but feelings the next minute.
I was raped last night
And sometimes
Just sometimes
I want to die.

The Stranger

While lying in bed, I start to cry.
If you were to ask the reason why,
I'd tell you I don't know who to be.
I can't free the stranger inside of me.
Right before bed, I did usual things,
Brushing my teeth and removing my rings.
And what I did next, if you should ask,
Was get into bed to remove my mask.
I can't discern right from wrong
So tell me, where do I belong?
All I can say, for a fact,
Is that I can't keep up this act.
If I could have a wish tonight,
I'd soar through the sky to an unknown height,
Like an eagle in its flight
Until the evening sky turns light.
I'd surely pay you any fee
If you would show me who to be.
I have a heavy cross to bear
And a large price to pay
For my childhood nightmares
That never went away.
I haven't been trying hard
Although I know I must
Dig a little deeper
And find a little trust.
But when tomorrow comes,
I'll have to do a task.

What? you ask.
I think you know.
I must put on my mask.
Goodnight
For now I must sleep or I will be in danger.
I can't bear another minute looking at this stranger.

Anguish

There is no rest for the tortured mind.
The troubled soul gets no reprieve.
Thought bumps into thought
And conflict is inevitable.
I ride a spinning wheel of feelings,
Never lingering with any emotion.
There is no closure.
I have unproductive energy.
Nothing is accomplished.
There are wars,
There is no victor;
It's another stalemate.
Chaos reigns.
No hope exists.
The life force is sucked out of me
And taking a shower is a monumental task.
This is the rule, not the exception.
I fight cutting my flesh.
I fight labels, ignorance,
And a poor prognosis.
I am fundamentally alone
With the cacophony of voices.
I want desperately to die.
But I tighten my grip
And hope for hope.

Expectations

I lost my everything
At least that's what I thought
When Daddy walked away
And left me so distraught.
The only hope I had
Was for his quick return.
I screamed in terror,
Banged the door.
Eventually, I'd learn.
I learned to be obedient.
I didn't cry or scream.
I sat alone with nothing
But what was a futile dream.
I longed for him to rescue
And release me from the shame.
I didn't realize
It was a sick and twisted game.
They'd break my forming self
And laugh as I would bleed.
It hurt to be a person
That meant to be in need.
You're just a hole, he said
As he raped me on that bed.
A table; I was wrapped in chains.
Many times I'd feel those pains
Choking on the doughnuts
Drowning in the liquor
I wanted them to kill me.
It would have been much quicker.
They said it was my fault.

You're too easy to adore
And then they'd tire of me
And push me to the floor.
I cried for their attention.
They kicked me in the face.
Seeing them with other girls
Filled me with disgrace.
I became what they expected
The perfect little whore.
I made myself into a blaze
That they could not ignore.

Love Touches Me (Or Not)

Love touches me
Or not.
But when it does, it chars.
Love touches me
But that's all.
It doesn't grip.
It grazes me
And slips away
And when it doesn't,
It suffocates.
Love touches me;
I touch sex.
I'll fuck you inside out.
Tell me how you want it.
But love?
Love?!
Well, come back another day.
Love touches me
Or not.
Or not.

The Damned

The child was born to suffer.
The child was made to grieve.
She lives with constant agony
That she cannot relieve.
The child is quite a genius.
She won't amount to much.
She has someone who loves her.
He's poisoned by her touch.
Give up your life, sweet child.
Forget your golden dreams.
We said if you would every leave
You'd crumble at the seams.
We let you go this far
But you know you must return
Or kill yourself,
You stupid bitch.
Oh, will she ever learn?

Price Tags

If only I could escape the pain.
It comes as part of the bargain.
You may choose to disregard the facts,
But when Satan hands you a package of tricks,
There is a price tag on each novelty:
Loss of peace and joy,
Dignity and self-respect,
An unquenched longing for meaning,
But there is only disillusionment.
Oh, to be able to wash the shame away,
To scrub it away,
To see it swirl down the drain like so much soapy water.
But you cannot.
And when you take off your mask at night,
You face it in the mirror.
It stares you down and mocks you.
You thought you could beat the system,
But you ignored the cost.

Reborn

I am just an empty shell
An inflatable doll
Breathe life into me.
I prefer not to bleed.
I don't like pain
But I'll bleed if I must.
I'll hurt for you.
The nothingness is unbearable.
Worship me.
I have something you need.
Bleed me.
Affirm I'm alive.
I'm disgraced and broken.
But I go on.
And I go on.
And the blood flows
And I'm reborn
And I choke on the tears.

Damaged

I am lost in a bottomless reservoir of need.
Like an insect trapped in amber,
There is no release.
I am ravenous;
I stalk and am not satisfied.
I am like a pearl cast to the swine.
I was a china cup in careless hands
Having been dropped, shattered, and glued together,
I was placed on a shelf with a sign reading,
Damaged Goods
I thirst for love
But pain, not love, washes over me
In my reservoir of craving.

Wilderness So Wild

My heart is in a cage
That's full of pain and rage.
I have no need for love
Or anything thereof.
I have no need at all
Not since I took the fall.
So look the other way.
I have no more to say.
I want your love so much.
I don't think you can touch
This wilderness so wild.
Love died inside this child.

The Cliff

The emptiness sears.
The blood flows.
The pain I feel
Nobody knows.
I wish to die.
Please let me go.
I have no hope
Of healing release.
I've spent my life
In search of peace
It has eluded me through the years.
I cannot bear more buckets of tears.
What cruel torture
God had in store
When Mom and Dad
Came together before.
I belong to evil.
I have no choice.
They stole my future
And silenced my voice.

The Pact

Enough--
It's a foreign concept.
I cannot possess enough.
My pores are like a sieve
Through which enough is sifted
Until there is a void.
Your penis cannot fill me enough.
Come one, come all.
I invite the masses to ravage me
With a collective prick.
But mere men cannot appease
My insatiable longings.
Sold to The Beast,
My heart is bound by a seemingly unbreakable,
Insoluble pact with him.
I cry tears of blood
As his nectar drips from my center.
Don't turn away.
Love me together
Until the holes are plugged
And it is enough.

Payoffs

I find that I cannot ignore
The fact that I am on the floor.
Addiction's running through my veins.
I can't shake the withdrawal pains.
I wonder if I'll soon find peace
And see illusions crash and cease.
I live my life and do what's right
But then I fall into this plight.
It may seem strange that I seek chaos
But it does provide some payoffs.
Because I have been acting wild
I may be carrying a child.
It's quite a seductive viper
Now I'll have to pay the piper.

The Marionette

I'm a puppet on a string.
Turn me any way you like.
I'm inanimate.
Twirl me; watch me dance
And be your social butterfly.
I'm trapped by old habits.
I want so much to be loved.
But I'm tired.
I just find it easier
To let you pull my string.

A Fresh Look At Love

Love, to me, is tears falling from the eyes like blood flows freely from an open wound.
It tears at the souls of the weak, ruthlessly shredding any dignity.
They say that love is what makes the world go 'round.
If that's the case, give me a one-way transfer ticket.
For love has shown me no kindness.
I've only met with deceit and betrayal.
I laugh in my face for being an utter fool and withdraw from love for infinity
Until another scab breaks and the tears fall--then I'll know it must be love.
And so I'll put a bandage on my heart, wipe away the tears, and, being the victim, fall again.

Twisted Nursery Rhyme

Red, red
The man is dead.
A head
It bled
I'm filled with dread.
Red, red
I should be dead.
A pill
A drink
Something so I cannot think.
Anything
Don't make me think
Of how I hurt
Of how I ache
There's not much more that I can take.
Red, red
Head
Bled
Enough said.

Trapped

Shiny armor,
Thick and seemingly impenetrable,
Surrounds my heart.
My soul cries
But no sound is heard.
The walls are too sturdy.
God, can you hear?
No one can help me; can you?
A tear trickles down my face.
H E L P
The sound echoes within the steel chamber
And within moments is squelched.
My soul is trapped
And I see no relief.

Pretty Little One

A girl is born.
For some, this is cause for celebration
(Not so for the girl).
She is pretty.
Her fate is fixed,
Her destiny sealed.
If she were ugly,
Her homeliness would be burdensome
But her life would be her own.
What a shame to be so pretty.
She's a slave,
Lovely ornamentation.
I'm sorry, pretty little one,
That soon you'll be sorry.

A Paradox

I'm empty and yet so full.
I merely exist.
Craving fulfillment, contentment,
Just one drop to assuage my parched soul
But the cup is dry--
Empty.
Yet I'm so full.
An abundant supply of pain and hunger;
I swirl in its fullness.
I'm drowning without a drop.
I'm full, overflowing.
Yet I'm so empty.

The Love Junkie

Cursed, the specter of love haunts me,
Boring into my soul with eyes like daggers, provoking.
Oh, won't you give me a fix?
With knuckles death-white, I cling to what little is my own.
We strike a bargain.
Give me your power.
I already have.
Sell me your soul.
It's already yours.
Then lay down your life.
The cruel voice reverberates in my skull, and I am hooked.
The bell tolls, and with my dying breath,
I become one with love.

Trust Is A Four-Letter Word

A little girl is abandoned in a world of nightmares.
Her heart races frantically as her eyes drown all that she sees.
Promises aren't made to be broken.
Years later, she's a superficial young woman,
Deceived and used for all she's worth.
A mask of happiness shields her face.
An insurmountable wall between her
And the outside world still exists,
Behind which promises don't keep
And trust is a four-letter word.
Underneath, she's just a sad child,
Waiting for a knight in shining armor
To gallantly take each brick from the evil wall
And set her free.
Trust is a four-letter word
Promises aren't made to be broken.

The Lesson

Pain, ice-blue and unrelenting,
Pierces my inner core.
It is my schoolmaster, and I,
The intractable student,
Suffer the indoctrination.
I beg for relief, an antidote
But here is no remedy
To quell the agony
And I have no choice but to endure.
Endure, and embrace,
The tormenting hunger, void, and hurt.
And as I linger in my prison of pain,
I know there will be no parole.
I subject myself to the sentence,
And allow the blue spirit to envelop me.

The Dilemma

Black on white
Or white on black?
There is no clear answer.
A pristine life?
A vessel of innocence
Marred by those who couldn't appreciate her value
Or appreciated it all too well?
Or could it be that her altruism,
Springing from a seemingly pure heart,
Masks her true nature--
Anathema?
With bloody hands
She removes her wings, hanging them up for the night.
Forgive me, Father, for I have sinned.
Black on white?
White on black?
The jury is still out.

Reclamation

You're an evil child,
Demon seed.
You're wickedness personified
With fangs for teeth
The devil's mark
A pentagram upon your heart.
Don't cry to others.
They cannot hear
The wailing of the devil's spawn.
Keep the secret come the dawn.
There's no redemption for you,
No savior to come to your rescue.
You are chattel.
Taste the blood
And renounce God.
Renounce peace.
Renounce love.
You in that white gossamer gown.
You've no right to emulate purity.
Your innocence is gone.
We'll spoil you
And soil you.
Glory in the blood,
Covering satin and lace.
Revel in it.
Drink it up.
You're drinking from the devil's cup.
We'll plant his demons in your womb.
You'll steep in his nectar
Dripping from your center.

Strange child
I look in the mirror
And all that I see
Is a hurting child
No demon seed.
Hungry for affirmation
I knew nothing else.
I had no choices.
Like a citizen in a war-torn country
I did what I could to survive.
They offered communion in evil
They believed the lies themselves.
Pity
I looked for morsels of love
Kindness among the embers
But I found none.
When starved of food
A stone will suffice.
I'll peel the evil from my skin.
It never seeped within.
I reclaim peace
Reclaim love
Reclaim white
Reclaim light.

The Choice

Is it better to live or to die?
The dead have no pain.
They don't go insane.
They don't cry.
They don't ask "why?"
But they don't know love.
They don't feel the breeze.
They can't smell the flowers.
They can't see the trees.
They don't learn new skills
Or experience thrills.
So which is the desirable state?
If I were living,
I would say life.
But my whole being groans from the weight of death.
I didn't choose it
But it's become my inheritance.
I reclaim the life that was mine to own.
I taste its sweetness.
I see its beauty
And, at last, I affirm.
Life is for the living.
There is no choosing.

A Flourishing Wasteland

It's not that I want to die.
I really want to thrive.
But I don't.
I'm damaged.
How do I escape this wasteland,
A wasteland containing one flower?
You say, *At least one flower grows.*
Perhaps another will sprout.
I say, *Take your pie-in-the-sky attitude*
And file it under 'bullshit.'
Still, I wonder.
Maybe you're right.
But look at the destruction.
It's disheartening
And I've grown rather fond of this wasteland.
Well, sort of.
I've worked diligently to make this
The best damn wasteland there is.
Yet a flower grows.
I suppose I'll stay.
It's not as if I have a choice.
Not if I wish to thrive.

Little Girl

Little girl, you are so wondrous,
Such a precious jewel.
Why do you give up your love
To every passing fool?
They cannot appreciate the wonders you possess.
Why you sacrifice yourself is anybody's guess.
You took on the likeness of the grandma I abhorred.
You must know the agony of torture I endured.
Drop your guard and notice that the ones that you adored
Abused your body--something you can no longer afford.

An Object Lesson

You're very sexy.
What a face, you exclaim,
As you worship me.
But it's not me that you worship
And it's not worship at all.
It is my veneer, not my person that you value.
I could be anyone.
I am an object to you.
I need to be your object.
It would be better than being nothing at all.
Now if I can believe I am your everything
I can avoid the emptiness I feel--
Death of innocence
Death of control
Death of personhood
And death of God
I won't be a victim again
But what am I
When I take mere crumbs in place of sustenance
And fashion myself according to your whims?
When I say I want to be an object
I'm saying that I want to be a victim.
That's what I was to them long ago
An object
A victim
How is it different today?

The Metamorphosis

The caterpillar stirs, so slightly, from within his constricting abode, his shackles binding--stifling. He considers his former state: crawling close, almost clinging, to the ground, eating debris, never realizing that above his head flies the butterfly, free to explore the heights. But there comes a time when he can no longer be bound; he will be released to experience the unlimited freedom of which he had no previous knowledge.

I, too, crawled in the dust and not so long ago. And from within the ties that bind me to my former days, there is a ray of hope. In time, my shackles will bind no longer, and I will evolve, emerge, and be exposed to a life that I knew could exist for me if only I could escape mere survival. My colors will be beautiful, kaleidoscopic. You may not recognize me, unless perhaps you have stolen a glimpse of my imminent transformation as it unfolds within my chains.

I wait in anticipation of the metamorphosis.

Stalemate

You intrigue me.
You are golden, immutable.
With stealth, I will capture you.
My rooks will enslave your king,
And you will be mine.
Only how will you save me
When I've cornered you?
Stop talking to me.
You make me realize I don't know you at all.
I don't know your moves.
I am just a pawn.
I can't find my voice.
I lost it in a castle somewhere.
Maybe I'm the player.
Maybe your song can't free me
And I'm the golden child, holding the score.

Battle Scars

He marks me
KILLER
As I fidget.
I've told him that I am not like him.
He is more like me than he knows.
He speaks of the glory of violence.
He learned to like it.
He once saved my life.
He pushes me to join him in destruction
As I plead with him to join me in mercy.
He wouldn't have come
If I could kill
And, once,
I would have died
If he hadn't.
We share dissimilar views
But we share a body.
Sometimes I fear him
But I am always grateful for his sacrifice.

Broken Fragments

I stumbled and fell in a heap,
Watching dreams shatter into myriad pieces.
With the breaking, I felt my heart crumble as well.
There was a still, small voice:
I can do much greater things with you than can be imagined.
Shall we create a masterpiece from this pile of fragments?
I silently wrestled, looking at the shards of dreams.
I took them, grasping them tightly,
Fearing they would be whisked away.
But with a greater fear of what might happen
Should I not allow this healing work,
I reluctantly let go, afraid I would change my mind.
Then, thinking better of it,
I threw myself into God's arms as well.

Becoming

I couldn't leave until I could leave.
I had strength to crawl away.
I bid farewell to the
Mutual Abuse Society
That we created.
I need to love myself.
I need positive connections with others.
We had a positive thread
And a negative chain
Holding us together.
We don't hurt each other
Or ourselves like we once did.
Well, most of the time.
One day, I won't do me wrong.
You say it's just who you are.
I say it's who I am right now.
It won't be who I am
When I become what I'm becoming.
And what I'm becoming is whole.

Scary Tales

Somebody go tell Cinderella.
There aren't any princes.
She must be tired of waiting by that window.
Put the gown away.
The slipper is irrelevant.
You're not a helpless waif
In someone else's fantasy.
The petulant child hurls the slipper
And collapses among yards of lace.
She needs no reminders.
Cindy, with your tattered rags and ashen face,
Leave your evil keepers.
Come into a safe place
Here within my heart.
Glass slippers fit in fairy tales
Not in real life.

Only Grace

I don't understand.
You see a masterpiece in scribble
Loveliness in wreckage
Must be like those funhouse mirrors
All green flame and wizards.
I don't understand.
Your voice becomes soft;
I hear only gibberish
The Tower Of Babel in our living room
A foreign film without subtitles.
You want to touch me,
To explore my terrain
I know you would be tender and kind.
You don't understand.
I don't want you to see my shame
To touch my disgrace.
I am like one whose home has been violated
Wrought-iron gates, a watchdog
Alarm set
Watching TV in the darkness
Startled when the house settles.
I want to give myself completely
Without terror and endless grief.
What will I see in your mirror?
I'd like to peel back my shame
And see only grace.

Freed From Shame

He touches me with the touch of a lover
But I feel the touch of another.
A monster
My father
And countless others like him;
Soul killers
I implode
As I fall into an abyss.
I am without core.
I feel loss of self.
Sadness overwhelms
And rage builds.
I hate myself sometimes
For being female
For being vulnerable
For simply being.
He touches me with love, my lover
But I still feel the touch of another.
Maybe, someday,
I won't see my father in his eyes
And my father's shame in me.
I need to know I'm okay now.
And maybe I can be freed from my shame.

1—2—3—You Don't Have Me

You think you're so smart.
You thought you had me.
Was it as easy as 1—2—3?
You may violate a body,
Maim and desecrate it.
You may coerce it to mechanically perform your will.
But there is something you didn't count on.
I am tenacious, resilient.
You can't kill my spirit.
You see, I love life.
And I know that love doesn't hurt.
Abuse does.
Love is beautiful, expansive, and restorative.
In that, you failed.
I am damaged.
My mind is cracked, though not broken.
And there is something you didn't count on.
With each day, I mend.
I will transcend the wickedness.
You occupy my mind,
But you will be evicted.
I have no room for you anymore.

Coming Home

I'm home. I haven't been here in quite awhile. There are cobwebs and empty cabinets.

I sit on the sofa and gaze at the snow. With a chill, I recall the treacherous journey--the hunger, fear, pain, numbness, the enemies encountered, striving to thwart me. At times, I followed the wrong path, my visibility minimal due to the storm. Many times, I slept in abandoned shacks, losing all hope of ever reaching my destination alive. But I trudged on. Overcome with weariness and desperation, I doubted myself. Did I even have a home? I turned against myself, and the possibility of rescue seemed remote. But I found my way. I had help; I won't take all the credit. But, in the end, it was I who saw the chimney, the smoke.

Now I am safe. I turn from the window and to the fire crackling in the fireplace. It warms the whole room.

Who started the fire? I did, when I refused to think of my trip as a lost cause and found the road leading home. I felt the warmth inside of me, and it spurred me on.

I walk to the cupboard and pull out two crystal goblets. I fill them with grape juice and toast myself.

A Poor Substitute

I recall what I once chose to forget.
I stood within a circle of men,
Vultures seeking carrion.
I didn't understand the game
But I'm a quick study.
Funny
I thought I wanted the ravaging.
Desperate for love,
I found crumbs in the wreckage.
I WAS the wreckage
And the love
I so desperately sought
Was hidden within my heart.
I was offered a poor substitute.
I won't settle anymore.

Growing Pains

I came seeking solace.
The tree spirits embraced me.
The park bustled with activity.
Wind bore ripples in the lake
As birds gathered for a meeting.
Butterflies skittered
And ants were on duty.
I chose a fallen leaf for a memento.
Sunlight dappled grass
While bikers biked
Walkers walked
And children ran with abandon, chuckling about something
Or nothing in particular.
I considered this cornucopia of life
And my place in it.
All follow a rhythm.
I must join the dance.
I fear my unfolding.
I am mindful of this moment
As present swiftly turns to past.
I can forsake regret
If I honor my own rhythm.

Power

You lacked power.
Hate drove your attempt to erase my uniqueness,
Your sense of helplessness translated into force.
True power is inner strength;
It is integrity
And the ability to contain impulse.
I feared your control.
Now I see weakness behind your force
And strength in my power.

Little Bird

Little bird with a broken wing--
She couldn't soar.
She couldn't sing.
The little bird could only cry
And if you were to ask her why
She'd say because she couldn't fly.
The little bird became quite scared.
She wasn't sure she was prepared.
She wondered why she even cared.
The little bird said, with a sigh,
I'll test my wing.
I won't fly high.
For if I cannot touch the sky
I know that I will surely die.
I hope my wing will now comply.
She tried, and she fell
She wanted to hide
But she got back up
And spread her wings wide.
Flying higher and higher
Enjoying the ride
Over the sand and the ocean tide.
She now had reason to rejoice.
The little bird now had a choice
She sang out loud with a clear, strong voice.
And what a song it was.

Lunchtime Ponderings

The afternoon sun bakes my arms as I walk in solitude.
A spring breeze ruffles my hair.
I take in the fragrance of flowers
While honeybees play tag
And trees whisper greetings.
My steps sound on the pavement
And I hear children playing.
I realize I am never alone.
When I consider this handiwork,
I see my part in the scheme.
Marshmallow clouds roll overhead
Slowly but with direction.
While watching a moth glide through the air,
I consider how much more I am enveloped with splendor.
I am among God's wonders.

Crown Jewels

You're garbage, just waste, he said.
I was kneeling on concrete,
A thick metal chain dangling from my mouth.
They sat around a long metal table
Like a twisted Last Supper
They gathered to feast before the darkest day of the year.
A noxious odor rose from my plate.
He placed it in front of me.
Eat it! You're a garbage heap.
An unseen one pulled at the leash,
Forcing my mouth open.
I am not waste,
A human trash compactor
Nor am I a goddess
Fancy robes, special jewels
They didn't want me to know
I'm human.
They divorced their humanity.
If any one of them came to my door tonight,
Hungry and bleeding,
I would nourish them
And clean their wounds.
I've seen the darkest humanity.
I've embraced the goodness.
Love and kindness are the crown jewels.

The Prettiest Thing

What's the prettiest thing you can imagine?
A smile on a face?
A rose in a vase?
A dress made of lace?
Whatever it is,
I hope you can see it today.

Sweet Relief

Sometimes, the world is topsy-turvy.
News of a murder
Dangerous weather
A broken economy
Threatens my peace.
I find consistency in nature.
I know light will greet me in the morning.
Sweet slumber finds me in the darkness.
There won't be snow in June.
Tides roll in on schedule.
Spring brings new birth.
The Earth sighs.
Trees bear witness.
My spirit is renewed.
There is comfort amidst chaos.

Trees

In spring, trees offer an abundant array of flowers.
Come winter, they are barren.
We are often like trees.
In good times, we display joyfulness.
When our winter comes, we feel barren.
Sometimes, we question God,
Our arms stretched toward sky.
We wait for sustenance.
I believe that then God helps us,
Like trees,
To grow.

Special

You are truly special,
Just because you're you.
You may not believe it,
But it's really true.
You are truly special,
Just because you are.
Each and every one of us
Is a shining star.

Love Is

I love to learn.
I'm learning to love.
I once cast men in my drama,
Costumed in expectations.
We shared, not love,
But emotional dependency,
Half-souls seeking completion.
I am whole;
I love another
Souls bare, undisguised.
Half-souls rescue.
They therefore control.
Seeking salvation,
They are further lost.
It is not love that disables.
It is not fatal,
Offering little at grave cost.
Love is healing
And vast
And I bask in the knowledge.

Rising

I was the Anti-Midas.
You said everything I touched would turn to dust.
I once proved you right.
Now, I make the rules.
I had been afraid to speak
But you never told me not to write,
And you no longer silence me.
I live in serenity.
I don't seek chaos.
Grief fails to consume me.
I sit with it, breathe,
And watch it subside.
I'm the first to succeed.
You chose another path.
I struggle,
Yet I'm much more than a survivor.
I heal;
It's challenging.
At times, it's exhilarating.
I don't live in the box you created.
I've risen from the ashes.

Helpful Links

RAINN—Rape, Abuse and Incest National Network
www.rainn.org

SEX AND LOVE ADDICTS ANONYMOUS
www.slaafws.org

NATIONAL SUICIDE PREVENTION LIFELINE
www.suicidepreventionlifeline.org

SURVIVORSHIP—FOR SURVIVORS OF RITUAL ABUSE, MIND CONTROL AND TORTURE (AND PRO-SURVIVORS)
www.survivorship.org

INTERNATIONAL SOCIETY FOR THE STUDY OF TRAUMA AND DISSOCIATION
(There are survivor resources, including a link where you can find a therapist)
www.issd.org

Made in the USA
Columbia, SC
24 October 2020